Letts KS2

Success

Revision Guide

Lynn Huggins-Cooper

Science

Contents

Plants

Animals and ecosystems

Humans

Flowering plants

Flowering plants

Petal
The petal is often brightly coloured and scented to attract insects.

Leaf
The leaf acts as a 'food factory', using the energy from sunlight.

Root
The root carries water and **nutrients** (goodness) from the soil to the plant, and keeps it anchored in the ground.

Did you know that we ate flower buds, roots and stems in our stir-fry last night?

That's funny – I thought we had broccoli, carrots and celery...

What is inside a flower?

A flower has male and female parts. The **pollen** is held on the male parts of the flower. It is the yellow or orange powder that you see at the centre of many flowers.

The pollen enters the female parts of the flower when it is carried there by insects, the wind, or even other animals.

The female parts of the flower contain the parts that will become seeds once **pollination** has taken place.

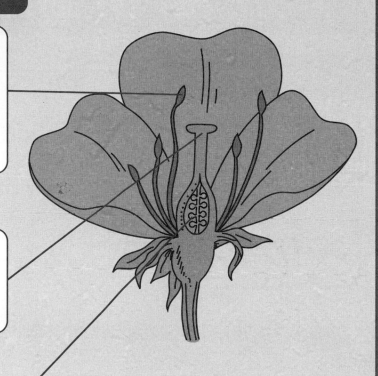

 **Top Tip** *You can see the internal parts of a flower really clearly in big flowers such as lilies. Have a look!*

Have a go...

Tell someone about the parts of a flower and what they do. Use a real plant to help you to explain.

Key words

petal	leaf
root	pollen
nutrients	pollination

Quick Test

Choose the best word to complete the sentences:

1 The root / stem / petal carries water and nutrients from the soil to the plant and holds the plant in the soil.

2 The root / petal / leaf is brightly coloured to attract pollinating insects.

3 The plant makes its food using the energy from the sun. The food is made in the leaf / stem / root .

4 The female / male parts of the flower contain pollen.

5 The female / male parts of the plant contain the parts that will become seeds.

A transfer of energy

Photosynthesis

Most plants need light and water to grow. Plants use the light energy from the Sun to make food in their leaves. This process is called **photosynthesis**. 'Synthesis' as part of a word usually means 'make', and 'photo' usually means that light is involved. So the word photosynthesis means 'made using light'.

Make sure you understand what most plants need to grow – you may be asked in a test and it will help you to grow healthier plants!

That's funny – I shut Mel in a dark room and she was definitely green when *she* came out ...

Hurumph!

Plants need light

What happens to plants grown in the dark?

If you put plants in the dark, they turn yellow and grow slowly. They need the **light energy** from the sun to make their food. There is a special green chemical in their leaves called **chlorophyll** that helps them to do this.

If you grow a plant on a windowsill, the plant grows towards the light.

Grown without sufficient light and water: spindly growth and yellow, shrivelling leaves.

Grown with sufficient light and water: strong growth and green, plump, juicy leaves.

Have a go...

Cut a piece of thick paper in the shape of the first letter of your name. Stick it to the top side of a big leaf on a growing plant with sticky tape. Leave it for a couple of weeks and then remove it. Your letter will show up in yellow on the green leaf!

Key words

photosynthesis   chlorophyll
light energy

Quick Test

1 Which of the things in this list do plants need to grow healthily?

water   soil   light   fertiliser

2 The process that green plants use to make their food is called:

photography   phototherapy
photosynthesis

3 What is chlorophyll?

4 Describe a plant grown with enough water but not enough light.

5 Describe a plant grown without enough water.

How plants reproduce

Germination

Plants go through many different stages in their lives.

A seed needs moisture, air and the correct temperature to germinate or start to grow.

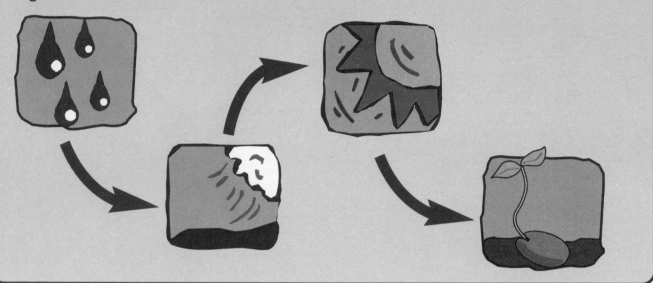

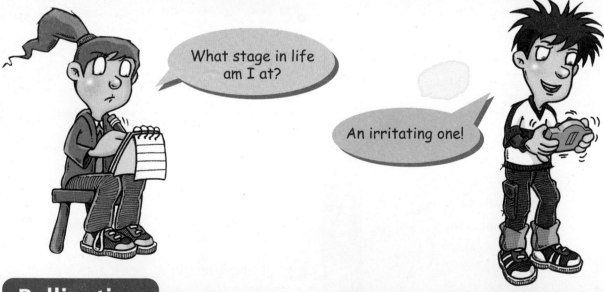

Pollination

Once the plant has grown and produced flowers, it may be pollinated. This is when the pollen from another plant of the same type has landed on the female parts of the plant. The **pollen may be carried on the wind or by insects.**

Fertilisation

The male cells in the pollen travel down a tube into the **ovary** of the plant and join the female cells. This is called **fertilisation** and it is how seeds are produced.

Some seeds such as blackberry pips and rosehips are spread by animals and birds when they eat the fruits.

Some seeds are specially **adapted** to grip onto fur and feathers.

Some seeds travel by water.

Some seeds blow on the wind.

The seed pods of the Himalayan balsam explode to scatter their seeds.

Top Tip For full marks, you should be able to remember all of the different ways that seeds can be carried around. Why not make up a *mnemonic* to help you?

Have a go...

Grow some sprouting seeds such as mung beans or adzuki beans in a jar on the windowsill. You can buy the seeds from health food stores. Put them in a jar and rinse them every day with clean water. They are lovely in sandwiches!

Key words

germinate	adapted
ovary	mnemonic
fertilisation	

Quick Test

1. Put these words into the correct order to describe the life cycle of a plant:

   pollination   germination
   fertilisation   seed dispersal

2. True or false?
   a Seeds need moisture to germinate.
   b Blackberry seeds are spread by explosions.
   c Some seeds are spread by water.

3. What do plants need to start to grow?

4. Describe three ways that seeds are spread.

5. Write a definition of 'pollination'.

Test your skills

Plant investigation

Two of these plants look worse for wear.

Have they been looked after properly? Can you guess what went wrong? Perhaps the plants have not had enough water or enough light. Can you tell which is which?

If you do not know now, then you will do after doing this investigation!

What you need

Three plants.

They must be the same size for this to be a fair test. Seedlings grown from sunflower seeds are a good choice – not your mum's best geraniums! Sunflower seeds can be sown in containers on the windowsill at any time during the year.

- Somewhere dark – a cupboard
- Somewhere bright – a windowsill
- A watering can and water

Three labels – marked 'Plant 1', 'Plant 2' and 'Plant 3'

plant 1

plant 2

plant 3

What to do

- Put a label on each plant pot.
- Put plant 1 in a dark cupboard and keep the soil moist.
- Put plant 2 on a windowsill and keep it moist.
- Put plant 3 on the same windowsill, but leave the soil to dry out.
- Write down what you think will happen to the plants.
- Leave them where they are for a week, making sure the soil for plant 1 and plant 2 is kept moist.

What happened? Were your predictions correct?

Test your knowledge

Section 1

Fill in the missing words from the box below:

root
petal
leaf
pollen
stem

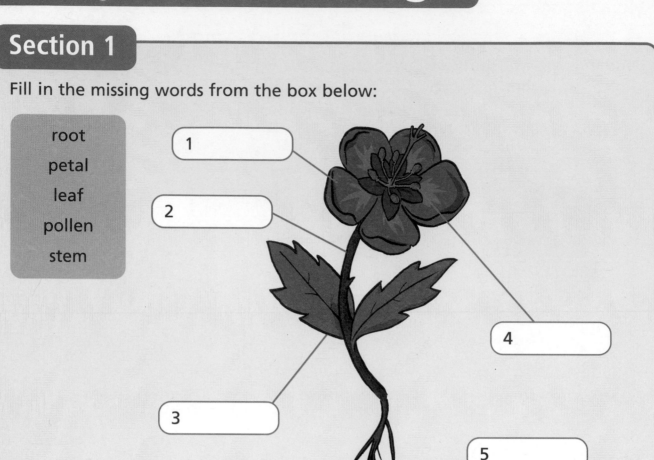

1
2
4
3
5

Section 2

Join each plant to the correct description with a line.

Plant grown in bright sunlight, plenty of water

Plant grown in the dark, plenty of water

Plant grown in bright sunlight, not enough water

Section 3

Put a ring round the correct answers.

1 What does a seed need to germinate or start to grow?

| moisture | cold | wind | air | correct temperature | birds |

2 Plants may be pollinated by:

| insects | slugs | wind | sunshine |

3 Seeds are spread by:

| wind | water | rain | birds | animals |

| sunlight | explosions |

Top Tip
Learn the names of the parts of a plant in the same way as you learn spellings – look, write, cover, check.

I never knew wind was so useful!

Me neither! I thought it just pushed clouds along!

Growing and changing

Changes...

All living things change as they grow. Some creatures change more than others.

Frog timeline: A frog starts its life as an egg in a blob of jelly called frogspawn. It emerges as a tadpole and gradually grows into a tiny frog.

frog spawn   tadpole   froglet   frog

Ladybird timeline: A ladybird starts life as a tiny yellow egg. When it hatches, it looks like a piece of black tyre rubber covered in bumps. Eventually the **larva** develops into a **pupa**. Inside the hard case, the creature is changing into an adult ladybird.

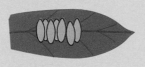   

eggs   larva   pupa   ladybird

It's a shame boys don't go through metamorphosis. Sam could do with undergoing a 'great change'!

Cheek!

14

More changes...

Chicken timeline: A chicken starts life as an egg. It hatches as a downy chick, then grows into a long-legged, skinny pullet. Finally, it grows into an adult chicken.

egg

chick

pullet

chicken

Human timeline: A baby is tiny and helpless when it is born. It then grows into a child. The child grows taller and changes through a process called **puberty** into an adult.

Metamorphosis

Some creatures go through a **complete change** as they grow. The young creature looks nothing like the adult. Animals such as frogs, ladybirds, dragonflies, butterflies, toads and newts come into this group. The change is called **metamorphosis**.

Top Tip

Remember the word metamorphosis by thinking about something in a film or videogame that changes before your eyes into something completely different – by MORPHING.

'Meta' means 'great' and 'morph' means 'change', so metamorphosis means 'great change'.

Have a go...

Search 'metamorphosis' on the Internet. Can you make a list of creatures that metamorphose as they grow? Make a file of photographs of creatures in the process of metamorphosis.

Key words

larva	puberty
pupa	metamorphosis

Quick Test

1. Explain what 'metamorphosis' means.
2. Name four animals that metamorphose.
3. What are frog eggs called?
4. What is the correct order for these words in the life cycle of a frog?

   froglet   frog   tadpole   frog spawn

Using classification keys

What are classification keys?

Classification keys are used to **classify** or sort things into groups. In biology, plants and creatures are classified into different groups according to **characteristics** that they share. Crabs and lobsters share the characteristic that they both have shells, for example.

Classification keys ask a series of simple questions to help you to **sort things into groups**. The questions are usually about some characteristic that a plant or creature has or does not have.

A group of things to be classified:

| crab | cat | butterfly | cabbage | bird | tree |

Two examples of classification keys:

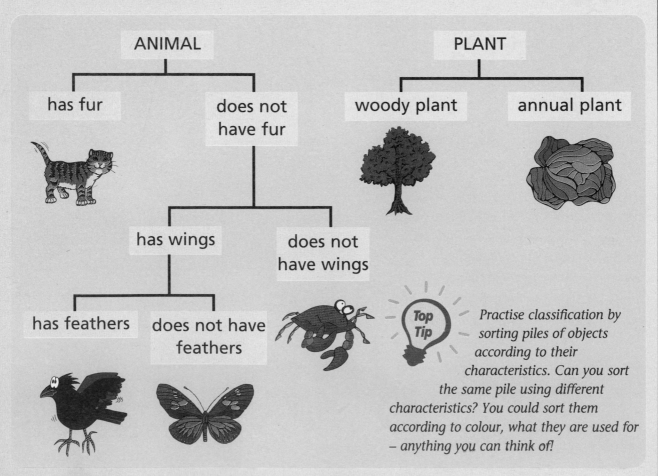

Practise classification by sorting piles of objects according to their characteristics. Can you sort the same pile using different characteristics? You could sort them according to colour, what they are used for – anything you can think of!

Venn diagrams

Venn diagrams are another way of sorting things into groups. They are used in maths as well as science.

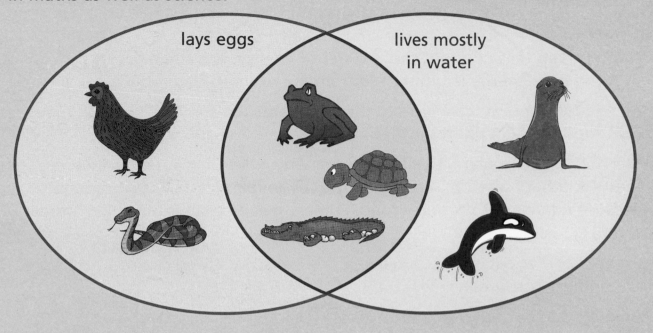

lays eggs

lives mostly in water

When creatures or plants could be members of both sets, they are placed in the middle part where the circles are joined. Alligators, turtles and frogs live mostly in water, and also lay eggs, so they are members of both sets.

Have a go...

Cut two paper circles and then cut pictures from magazines or comics to show someone how a Venn diagram works. Choose two characteristics to classify or sort your pictures into groups and show at least one example that is a member of both sets.

Perhaps I could use classification to help me sort out all of my CDs...!

But 'rubbish' and 'dreadful' are probably the same sets...

Key words

classification key   characteristics
classify   Venn diagram

Quick Test

Make up a classification key to sort out the following creatures and plants:

| duck | cow | hen | pig |
| daisy | turnip | fern | oak tree |

Food chains

Energy transfer

A **food chain** tells us **about the transfer of energy**. It is the simplest way of showing how energy is transferred from **organism** to organism.

All energy comes originally from the sun. Plants use sunlight to make their own food through **photosynthesis**.

In a food chain, a plant is called a **primary producer**, because it produces food for other creatures. Remember this by thinking that it is a producer, because it makes or produces food. Primary means it comes first, like primary school.

An animal that eats plants is called a **herbivore**. In a food chain, a herbivore is a **primary consumer**.

Animals that eat other animals are called **carnivores**. In a food chain, predators are called **secondary** or even **tertiary consumers**, because they come second or third. They are called predators, because they kill other animals and eat them.

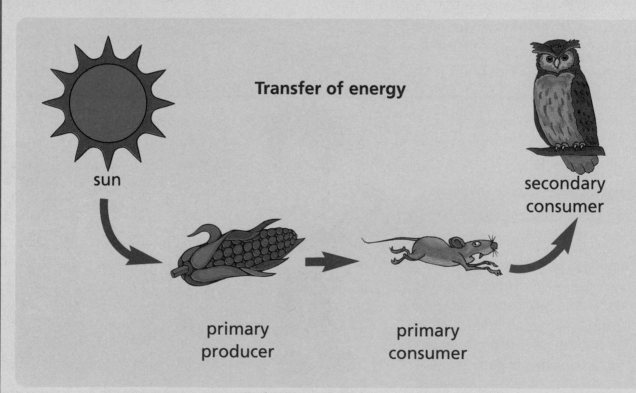

Transfer of energy

sun

secondary
consumer

primary
producer

primary
consumer

In the food chain, sun – corn – fieldmouse – owl, the corn is the primary producer, the fieldmouse is the primary consumer, and the owl is the secondary consumer.

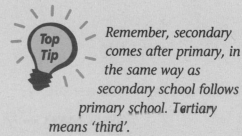

Top Tip

Remember, secondary comes after primary, in the same way as secondary school follows primary school. Tertiary means 'third'.

Food webs

A **food web** is more complicated. It involves connected food chains.

In a food web made up from dandelion, rabbit, fox, snail, thrush, the fox may eat the rabbit, but also may eat the thrush and even the snail. The web looks like this:

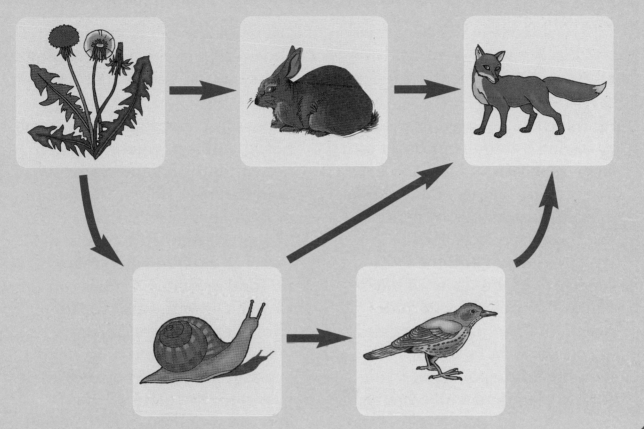

Have a go...

Make a food chain mobile from card and thread. Start with the sun at the top and join it with thread to a plant. Join the plant to a plant eater, then something that eats the plant eater – a carnivore.

Key words

food chain	carnivore
organism	secondary consumer
primary producer	tertiary consumer
herbivore	food web
primary consumer	

Quick Test

1   Put these in order to show a seaside food chain:

> seaweed   sun   shark   cod

2   Match the labels to the plants and animals in this food chain:

1 primary producer	**a** hedgehog
2 secondary consumer	**b** sun
3 primary consumer	**c** slug
4 energy source	**d** lettuce

Animals in their environment

How they adapt

Wherever animals live, they have to adapt to their **environment**.

Animals who live in the desert, where it is very hot and dry, and animals who live in the Antarctic, where it is very cold and bleak, are very well **adapted** to their harsh environments. If they were not, they would be unable to survive.

Penguins are adapted to the cold by having a **thick layer of fat to keep them warm**. They also have fine, downy feathers underneath their sleek, waterproof feathers. The fluffy layer acts like an insulating duvet and the waterproof outer layer of oily feathers acts like a waterproof jacket. The penguins sometimes seem clumsy on land, but their streamlined shape makes them acrobatic and graceful swimmers.

Camels are adapted for life in the hot, dry desert, where they can go without food and water for long periods of time. The hump on a camel's back is a fatty lump of flesh developed **to allow the camel to survive when there is no food or water**. Camels can survive without water for up to two weeks! They also have leathery eyelids and long, silky eyelashes to help to protect their eyes from the glare of the sun and the stinging sand. Their feet are flat and splayed, giving them a **large surface area**. These act like snowshoes, helping the camel to walk without sinking into the sand.

The Peppered Moth story

Animals adapt to their environment. This means that they change over time to make themselves fit in with the conditions in the place where they live.

The Peppered Moth is a good example. These common moths live in towns and in the country. In the country, they are a creamy white colour with speckles on their wings. In the city, Peppered Moths have much darker grey wings. This colouring has developed to help to **camouflage** them, to keep them safe from **predators** such as birds. The darker wings blend in with the grime and pollution found on many city surfaces where the moths settle.

Top Tip

Look at your pet or an animal you see on the television. How is it adapted to its natural environment or way of life?

I wonder if my maths teacher is adapted to life in freezing conditions? He's very hairy!

Yeuck!

Have a go...

Can you describe how a polar bear is adapted to life in freezing conditions? Do some research on the Internet to find out more.

Quick Test

Read the description of the planet Plaaarp and design an alien adapted to the environment.

My planet is Plaaarp! It has three glittering purple suns that shine all the time, so it is very hot. The ground is soft and slushy with the delightful texture of rotting peaches. Water drops from the sky constantly.

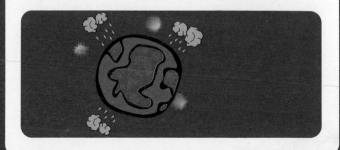

Key words

environment	camouflage
adapted	predators

Living processes

The seven processes of life

There are seven life processes that all living things share.

 They all feed

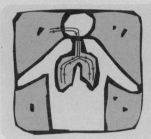 They all breathe

 They all move

 They all get rid of waste

 They all feel things

 They all grow and change

 They all produce young

 I do all those things – I must be alive!

 You don't have feelings, do you?

Is it alive?

Deciding if things are alive can be difficult.

It could be hard to decide whether plants were alive if you did not already know. You cannot usually see a plant move (not counting swaying in the wind). Plants do move though, to follow the light. If you grow seedlings on a windowsill, they will bend towards the light. So plants are alive.

Cats are alive – we know that from common sense. If, however, we had to explain to an alien, for example, why a cat is alive, we could say that the cat:

- eats
- breathes
- produces young – kittens!
- moves
- gets rid of waste
- feels things
- grows and changes

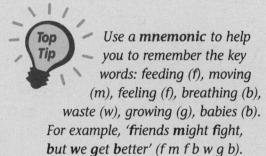

Top Tip

Use a **mnemonic** to help you to remember the key words: feeding (f), moving (m), feeling (f), breathing (b), waste (w), growing (g), babies (b). For example, 'friends **might** fight, **but we get** better' (f m f b w g b).

Have a go...

See if you can remember all seven things that show something is alive. Look at this web page for a fun activity to help you.
http://www.bbc.co.uk/schools/revisewise/science/living/03_act.shtml

Key words

mnemonic

Quick Test

Which of the things in this list are alive?

Explain to an adult how you made your decision.

1. Cat
2. Stream
3. Cactus
4. Spider
5. Star

Microorganisms

What is a microorganism?

A **microorganism** is a very **tiny, living thing**. You can work out that it has to be really small from the prefix 'micro'– because you will need a microscope to see it. Microorganisms include things such as **bacteria**, **viruses** and **fungi**.

Microorganisms can be harmful to people.

Viruses

Viruses, commonly called germs, make people ill.

- measles
- flu
- mumps

These illnesses are all caused by microorganisms called viruses.

Bacteria

Bacteria can also make people ill. Bacteria can cause stomach upsets and even food poisoning. That is why food hygiene is so important.

- salmonella
- gastroenteritis
- ear infections

These illnesses are all caused by microorganisms called bacteria.

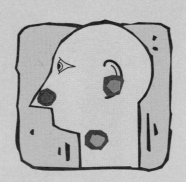

Fungi

Some fungi, such as the green mould that attacks bread, are also harmful, because they cause food to spoil and can make people ill if they eat it.

Helpful microorganisms

Yeast is used to make beer and bread. Bacteria are also used in the production of yoghurt.

beer   bread   yoghurt

The microorganisms that help to rot down compost are also helpful, because they break down waste such as fallen leaves and dead animals.

Top Tip
Remember, a microorganism is very small, so you cannot see it without a microscope. Even if your hands look clean, they can still be teeming with microorganisms – so always wash them before you eat!

 So bacteria can be really useful?

Yes... so why does Mum make us wash our hands?

Have a go...

Design a poster to encourage people to remember hygiene when they are preparing food. Look at this website for information:
http://archive.food.gov.uk/heal/index2.html

Key words

microorganism   virus
bacteria   fungi

Quick Test

1 How can microorganisms be helpful to people?
2 Name three harmful effects of microorganisms.
3 Name an illness caused by a virus.
4 Name an illness caused by bacteria.
5 Name a food made using bacteria.

Looking at habitats

What is a habitat?

Habitat is a word used to describe the place where a **collection of plants and animals live.** Habitats include such places as the seashore, forest, garden, wasteland, jungle and desert.

Community is the name given to **the animals and plants that live together in a particular place**.

An **ecosystem** is the scientific term that **describes the community and its habitat.**

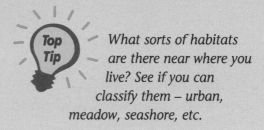

Top Tip

What sorts of habitats are there near where you live? See if you can classify them – urban, meadow, seashore, etc.

The great web of life

Creatures and plants living within a particular habitat, such as a tropical rainforest, are all linked in a great web of life. They also compete with each other for food, and only the strongest, best-adapted creatures survive and breed.

In the tropical rainforest, food chains and webs help to maintain **the balance of nature**. An increase in the numbers of animals is limited by the amount of food available.

Life in a community

There are always more organisms at the bottom of a food web than at the top. This is because the energy passed along is reduced with each link in the food chain. All life in a community is linked, so if for some reason one **species** is wiped out – say a disease killed all the rodents in the forest – **the rest of the community would be affected**. The carnivores would have to compete more for food and some could die through starvation. The nuts and seeds no longer eaten by the rodents would grow into trees and shrubs, and smaller species of plants could die through lack of light as they are covered by the large growth.

I'm off hunting for a fierce, top predator in a dangerous and complex ecosystem!

Looking for the cat again, are you?

Have a go...

What do you think might happen to the hedgehog population in a garden habitat if all the slugs and snails were killed off by poisoning?

Key words

habitat	ecosystem
community	species

Quick Test

Match the word to its correct definition:

1	habitat	a	place where a collection of plants and animals live
2	ecosystem	b	a tropical habitat
3	rainforest	c	animals and plants that live together in a particular place
4	community	d	meat eaters
5	carnivores	e	scientific term to describe a community and its habitat

Test your skills

The amazing woodlouse sorting machine!

What conditions do woodlice prefer? You are going to carry out an experiment to find out.

You need:

- Cardboard box, such as a shoebox
- Two extra cardboard sheets
- Plastic bag
- Soil
- Transparent food wrap
- Woodlice

What to do

- Cut a doorway in the centre of the two pieces of extra cardboard sheet.
- Stick the extra card down so it makes two rooms in the shoebox, with a corridor in the middle (see diagram on page 29).
- Line the bottom of each half of the box with a piece of plastic cut from the bag, to stop the cardboard going soggy.
- Put dry soil in each side of the box, then dampen one side.
- Put several woodlice in the corridor in the centre of the box, then cover the top of the damp end with pierced card so that it is dark, and cover the other end with pierced, transparent food wrap, so it is light.

 Top Tip

Be careful not to harm the woodlice and put them back where you found them as soon as you have finished your experiment.

Diagram

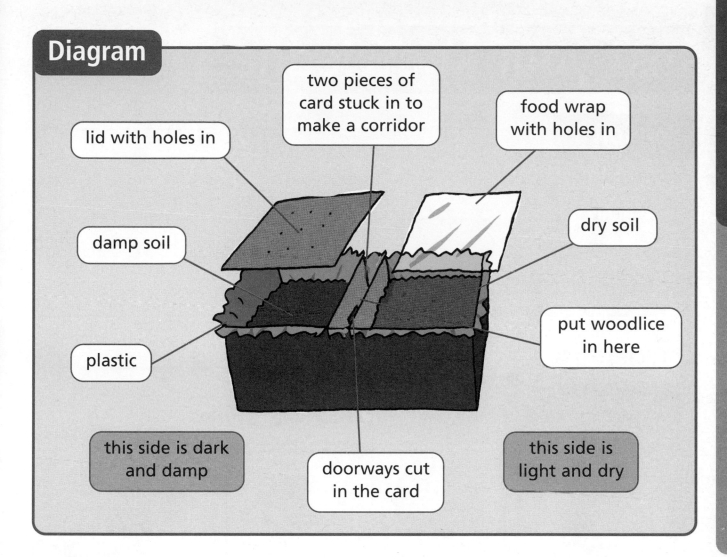

two pieces of card stuck in to make a corridor

food wrap with holes in

lid with holes in

dry soil

damp soil

plastic

put woodlice in here

this side is dark and damp

doorways cut in the card

this side is light and dry

Results

The woodlice will go to the place with the most comfortable conditions. You could repeat the experiment with four sections in your box – so you had:

- damp + dark
- damp + light
- dry + dark
- dry + light

Try to predict where the woodlice will go – then see if you are right!

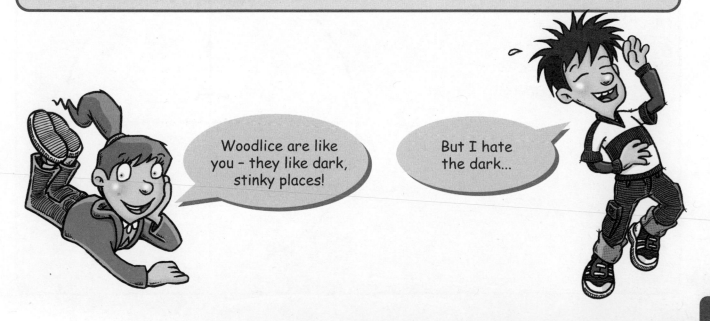

Woodlice are like you – they like dark, stinky places!

But I hate the dark...

Test your knowledge

Section 1

What is a:

1 Habitat _____

2 Community _____

3 Ecosystem _____

Section 2

1 Match the label to the correct picture in this food chain:

secondary consumer

top carnivore

primary consumer

primary producer

2 Draw the life cycle of a frog in the circle below. What is the process that means 'great change' called?

_____

Section 3

How is a beaver adapted to life in and around a river? Tick the correct boxes.

☐ Thick, waterproof fur   ☐ Thin tail

☐ Fine, thin silky fur   ☐ Tiny, sharp teeth for fighting

☐ Wide tail like a paddle   ☐ Large front teeth for gnawing wood

Section 4

Use the Venn diagram below to sort these animals into groups:

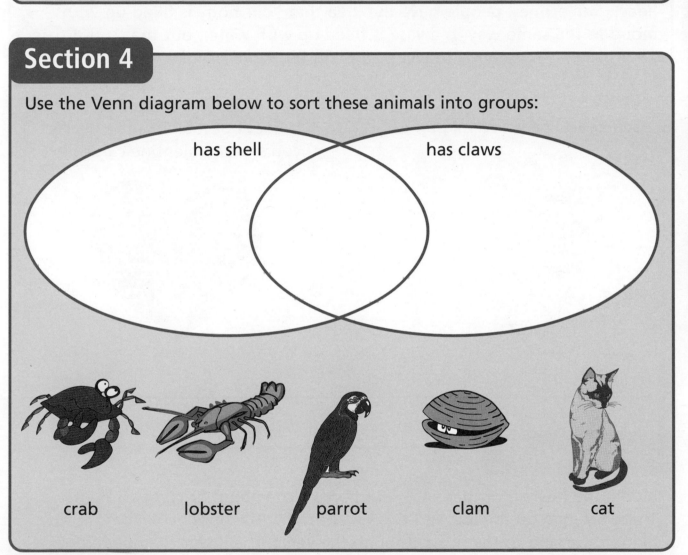

has shell   has claws

crab   lobster   parrot   clam   cat

Section 5

Match the microorganism to the correct result:

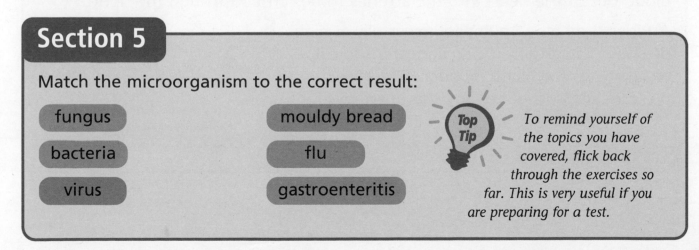

fungus   mouldy bread

bacteria   flu

virus   gastroenteritis

Top Tip — *To remind yourself of the topics you have covered, flick back through the exercises so far. This is very useful if you are preparing for a test.*

The circulatory system

The circulatory system

Have you noticed that when you cut yourself, blood wells up out of the cut, even after you have wiped it away? Have you ever wondered why it keeps appearing? The **circulatory system**, the name given to the system that moves blood around your body, is driven by a **very strong pump – your heart**. Sometimes, people have the idea that your body is filled up with blood in the same way as a vase is filled up with water, but that is not true. Your blood is constantly moving, carrying food and oxygen to all the cells in your body.

The heart is a powerful pump.

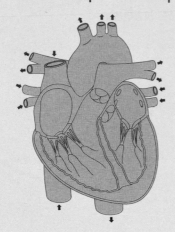

It does not look like the hearts you see on Valentine cards.

How it works

Inside, the heart is divided into four hollow 'chambers' or compartments. There are two on the left and two on the right. The upper chambers receive blood returning to the heart through the **veins**. The lower chambers force blood out of the heart into the **arteries** to be carried through the body.

Arteries carry blood pumped powerfully at high pressure. That is why it is so dangerous to cut an artery. As the blood is under so much pressure, it spurts out of any cuts in arteries.

Top Tip

It is easy to remember that arteries carry blood away from the heart, because 'art' is at the beginning of the word 'artery'.
He- art- ery

What is blood made up of?

We think of blood as a red liquid, but if you looked at blood under a strong microscope you would see several different things:

Red cells

These look like red saucers. They carry the dissolved oxygen around the body.

White cells

These attack invading microbes and fight disease.

Platelets

These are bits of dead **cells**. They clump together and help to clot your blood. When you cut yourself, platelets seal the hole to make a scab.

Plasma

This is the liquid that contains proteins, salts and sugars.

Did you know that when you do exercise, like in PE, your heart beats faster and your **pulse** rate goes up?

No, but I know that maths tests make my heart beat faster...

Have a go...

Make up a mnemonic to remind yourself what blood is made up of. For example:

- *rich (red cells) • women (white cells)*
- *please (platelets) • Pluto (plasma)*

Key words

circulatory system	
veins	platelets
artery	cells
red cells	plasma
white cells	pulse

Quick Test

1. Finish this sentence: Blood is made up of four parts:
2. How many chambers are there inside the heart?
3. Why is it particularly dangerous to cut an artery?
4. Which blood cells fight disease?
5. What is plasma?

Looking at teeth

Types of teeth and their job

Teeth are **tools for eating food** and in some animals they are also used for defence (or attack!).

Here are the teeth of three different animals. Look at the different shapes of the teeth.

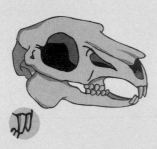

Large **incisor** teeth for cutting and cropping grass.

Sharp **canine** teeth for tearing food such as meat.

Flat **molars** for grinding and chewing food.

Herbivorous animals, such as those that eat grass, like sheep and cows, have flat, wide teeth for grinding and chewing tough stems. **Carnivorous** animals, like cats and dogs, have sharper, pointed teeth for tearing and chewing meat and sinews. These animals are often predators.

Your pet's teeth

Look at your pet's teeth. If you have a cat or dog, you will see they have teeth adapted for tearing and chewing meat. Look out for the sharp canines!

If you have a rabbit, guinea pig or hamster you will see they have teeth adapted to eating plants. Look out for their large incisors!

Caring for your teeth

You must take very good care of your teeth. Cleaning your teeth, using floss and mouthwash, helps to keep your teeth and gums free from the sticky **plaque** that causes decay. Plaque is caused by bacteria acting on the sugars left on your teeth after you have eaten.

You should also visit the dentist on a regular basis, so that he or she can check that there are no problems.

Top Tip

Eating cheese at the end of a meal can help to neutralise the acids in your mouth and reduce the chance of tooth decay occurring.

Would you like an apple?

Fangs a lot!

Have a go...

Design a leaflet describing how to keep your teeth healthy. Look at this website for ideas – and lots of fun: http://www.colgate.com/app/Kids-World/US/HomePage.cvsp

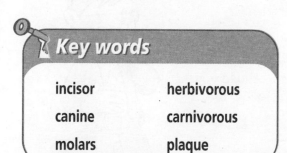

🔖 Key words

incisor	herbivorous
canine	carnivorous
molars	plaque

Quick Test

Match the type of tooth to the correct description.

1 canines — **a** teeth for grinding and chewing food

2 molars — **b** teeth for cutting and cropping grass

3 incisors — **c** teeth for tearing food such as meat

4 The Venusian Blargle eats grass and woody plants. Describe what sort of teeth they need.

5 The Venusian Blargle is hunted by a fierce predator, the Snortwoggle. What sort of teeth does a Snortwoggle need?

Looking at bones

Why do you have a skeleton?

Your skeleton has three jobs:

1 **Support**
   It stops you from flopping about. Your skeleton **acts like scaffolding** to prop up the soft tissues your body is made from.

2 **Protection**
   Your skull is a hard bony case that **protects your brain**. In the same way, your ribs protect your lungs and heart, and your pelvis protects many of your soft **internal organs**.

3 **Movement**
   Your bones are rigid, but the joints, together with the muscles, **help you to move** about.

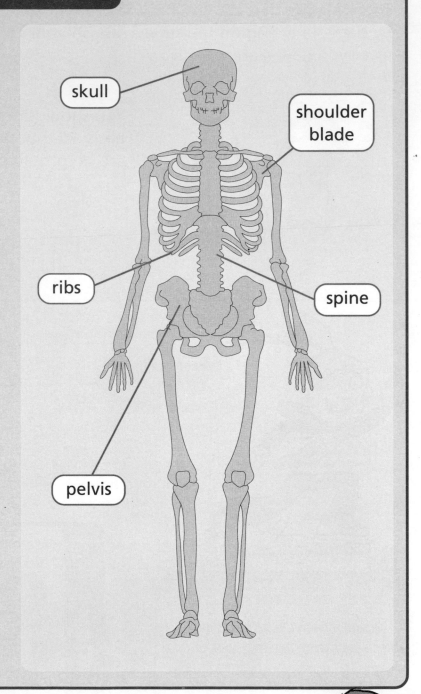

skull

shoulder blade

ribs

spine

pelvis

So it's because of my skull that it doesn't hurt when I head a football?

No, it's because you don't have a brain...

Joints and muscles

Have you ever bent your arm up and made a fist to show how big your muscles are? When you do that, you are moving a **hinge joint** at the elbow and you are showing how muscles tighten and loosen to make the arm work like a lever.

Find out more about what goes on inside your body here:
http://www.innerbody.com/htm/body.html

Muscles in your arm

To move your arm, different muscles have to work together.

When you bend your arm up to 'show your muscles', your **biceps** (bulgy muscle on the top side of your arm) tightens up and the smaller **triceps** on the underside of your arm relaxes. When you straighten your arm again, the opposite happens: your biceps relaxes and your triceps contracts.

biceps

triceps

Have a go...

Can you explain to someone what is happening when you 'show your muscles'? Can you tighten the muscles in your body and feel them under the skin? You could have fun tightening and loosening muscles in your face too – as long as no one thinks you are being rude!

Key words

internal organs	biceps
hinge joint	triceps

Quick Test

1. What are the three main functions of bones in our bodies?

2. Name the four major bones in the human body.

3. Fill in the missing words:

The _____ is the bulgy muscle on the top side of your arm.

The _____ is the smaller muscle on the underside of your arm.

4. What does your skull protect?

5. What do your ribs protect?

Eating healthy food

A healthy diet

We hear lots said about eating a healthy diet, but what does it really mean?
There are foods we should eat regularly to stay healthy.

We need:

Protein – in foods such as eggs, milk and cheese.

Carbohydrate – in pasta, bread and cereals.

Fats – in foods such as butter and cooking oil.

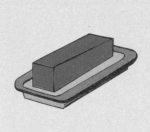

Fibre – in vegetables, fruit and cereals.

I run about a lot so I need lots of energy food!

One plate of pasta coming right up!

Food groups

Protein, carbohydrate, fats and fibre are called food groups. What job does each food group do?

- Protein is used by the body for building cells. Protein helps you to **grow and repairs damage** to the body.

- Carbohydrate is the body's **main source of fuel**. Carbohydrate gives you lots of **energy**.

- Fats are also a source of energy, but this is stored for times when you have no carbohydrate to burn.

- Fibre is needed to help you to **digest your food** and keep the whole of your **digestive system** in good working order.

Remember that some foods, such as those containing high levels of salt and fat, should only be eaten in small quantities.

 Have a go...

Look at your lunchbox or your dinner tonight. What food groups are you eating? Check out this website for more information on healthy eating: http://www.5aday.org/html/kids/kids_home.php

 Top Tip

Did you know that over 75% of your body is made up from water? That is why we need to drink plenty of healthy drinks such as water, juice and milk.

Key words

protein	fibre
carbohydrate	energy
fats	digestive system

Quick Test

Make up a picnic from the items shown in the picture above. Include foods from all the groups, i.e. protein, fats, carbohydrate, fibre.

Test your skills

KEEPING FIT AND HEALTHY

A lot of things happen to our bodies when we exercise.

Have you ever been out of breath after you have run about? This happens because **your muscles use up lots of oxygen when you exercise**. Your body needs oxygen quickly, so you breathe faster and more deeply.

You can also measure the effect of exercise by **taking your pulse**. When you are resting, your pulse beats at a normal rate. When you exercise, it gets faster. Once you stop, it returns gradually to the normal rate.

Pulse rate

Here is a graph recording Sam's change of pulse rate.

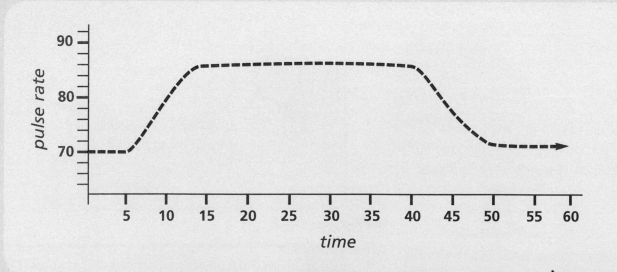

Sam has been playing basketball. See if you can tell from the graph when he started to play. Can you tell when his pulse rate returned to normal?

Find your own pulse

You can find your pulse by pressing down with the first two fingers of your right hand on the inside of your left wrist.

Using a watch or clock with a second hand, count how many beats you feel in a minute after resting, and write it down.

Then jump up and down until you feel puffed and count for another minute. Was there a difference? How long did it take for your pulse to slow back down to its normal rate?

Try different activities such as running, cycling and playing sports.

Which activity makes your pulse rate quickest? Why do you think this is?

Exercise makes me hot and sweaty!

I thought that was just called 'being a boy'...

Test your knowledge

Section 1

1 What are the food groups we need for a healthy diet?

_____

_____

2 Circle the healthier option in each pair:

apple   apple pie

grated carrot   carrot cake

fresh strawberries   strawberry jam

oranges   orange squash

Can you give reasons for your answers?

_____

_____

_____

3 Why do we need fibre in our diets?

_____

_____

_____

4 Draw a healthy dinner with food chosen from the basket below:

Section 2

1 Why do herbivorous animals, like sheep and cows, have flat, wide teeth?

_____

2 Why do carnivorous animals, like cats and dogs, have sharper, pointed teeth? _____

3 Circle the correct names of types of teeth:

incisor indicator omnivores

molar mole molecular

canine ceramic capillaries

4 What are the three functions of the skeleton?

_____

5 What are the names of the four things found in blood?

_____

6 Fill in the missing words:

Red cells carry _____ around the body.

White blood cells attack _____ and fight disease.

I'm no good at tests...

You're good at testing Mum's patience...

Looking at materials

What are materials?

The word **materials** describes **what items are made from**. A door may be made from the material wood, for example, and a window may be made from the material glass. Within your home, you will find items made from many different materials. Take a look and see how many you can identify!

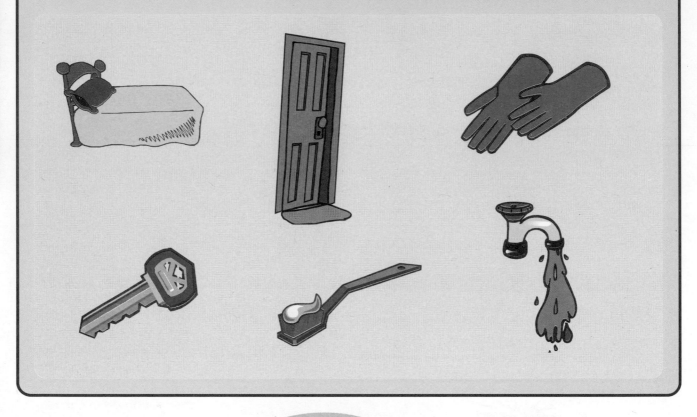

Choosing materials

When objects are designed, the materials they are to be made from are considered carefully. They are chosen according to the **characteristics of the materials** and the job they will be required to do. To get a picture of how important it is to choose the correct materials, consider the following:

A window made from fabric.

A door made from paper.

A mattress made from stone.

A chair made from glass.

What would be the problem with choosing these materials in each case? Ask yourself questions about the **properties** of each material and the job it has to do. Is it:

- hard/soft
- **pliable/brittle**
- **opaque/transparent**
- a heat conductor/not a heat conductor

Top Tip *Always try to think about the properties of each material and how this affects whether it is chosen during the design of an object.*

Have a go...
Look around your room – how many different materials can you see? Why do you think they were chosen?

Key words
materials	brittle
properties	opaque
pliable	transparent

Quick Test

1 How many materials can you identify in the picture?

2 Why do you think each particular material was chosen?

Filtration

Problem-solving

It is useful to think about the properties of materials when you have a problem to solve. Imagine you have a younger sister or brother who wants to play in their paddling pool, but the pool is full of leaves and broken twigs. You could pick out every piece by hand – but it would take you a very long time!

Alternatively, you could use a scientific approach and clean out the pool using **filtration**.

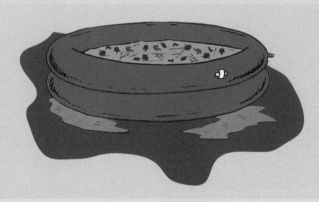

What is a filter?

A filter is the material used to separate out the different parts of a mixture. If you use a net to pick leaves and debris out of a pool, you are using filtration. The net is acting as a filter, separating the leaves from the water.

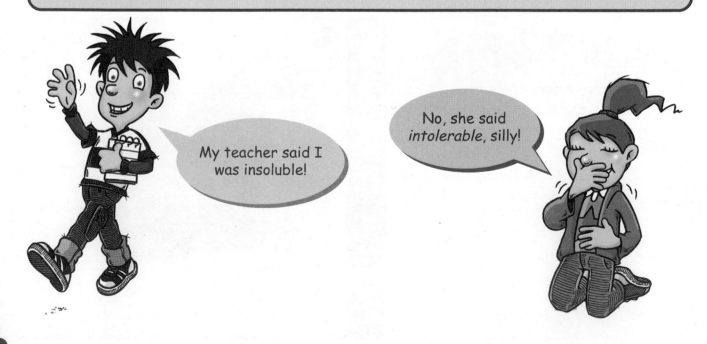

My teacher said I was insoluble!

No, she said *intolerable*, silly!

Separation

Filtration is used wherever the solids to be separated from the liquid are **insoluble** – will not **dissolve** in the liquid. Filtration would be used to carry out an experiment at school, if you were asked to separate sand from water.

What equipment would you choose? You know that sand is insoluble in water, so you would choose equipment to filter the mixture.

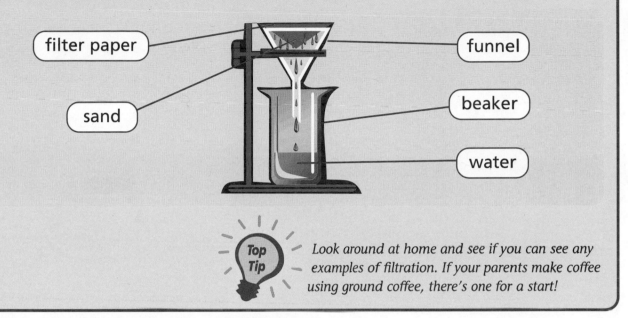

filter paper

funnel

sand

beaker

water

Top Tip

Look around at home and see if you can see any examples of filtration. If your parents make coffee using ground coffee, there's one for a start!

Filtration around the house

Look for examples of filters around the house. How many can you find? There are lots in the kitchen – tea bags, coffee filters, tea strainers, sieves – see how many more you can find!

Have a go...

Can you remember what properties of materials means? If not, look it up in the glossary at the back of this book!

Key words

filtration   dissolve

insoluble

Quick Test

1 What word is used to describe material that will not dissolve in a particular liquid?

2 What word describes the process of separating a solid that does not dissolve from a liquid?

3 What equipment would you choose to separate grit from water?

Draw a labelled diagram.

Materials that dissolve

Dissolving

When we say that a material has **dissolved**, we mean that it is **soluble** – it will combine with a liquid. Think of gravel in water and sugar in coffee. It does not matter how much we **stir or heat** the water with the gravel in it – the gravel will not dissolve.

When, however, we put a spoonful of sugar in a cup of coffee and stir, the **sugar gradually combines with the coffee** – we can no longer hear it grinding on the side of the cup. This is because it has dissolved.

Think also about tasting sea water when you are swimming. You cannot see the salt in the water, as it is dissolved – but you know it is there from the salty taste.

So when you make coffee, the sugar dissolves in the liquid.

I don't have sugar in my coffee. I'm sweet enough already!

Evaporation

On page 46 you read about **filtration**. **Evaporation is another way of separating materials**. Unlike filtration, **evaporation can separate dissolved solids from liquids**. The liquid is heated and as the **water vapour** (steam) rises (see *Reversible changes* on page 50), it hits a cold surface and changes back into a liquid. This process is called **condensation**. The liquid is then collected in a beaker. This carries on until all that is left behind in the original container is the solid.

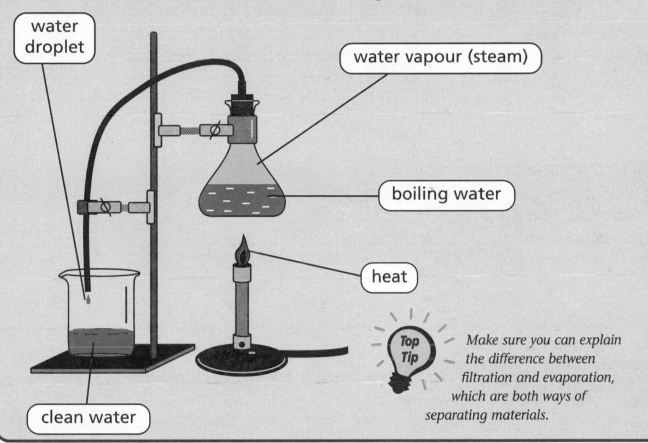

water droplet

water vapour (steam)

boiling water

heat

clean water

Top Tip

Make sure you can explain the difference between filtration and evaporation, which are both ways of separating materials.

Have a go...

Collect some solids from the kitchen food cupboard (NOT the cleaning cupboard, as some kitchen cleaners are dangerous) and stir them into a cup of water. Do they dissolve? Does it make a difference if you use warm tap water?

Key words

dissolved	evaporation
soluble	water vapour
filtration	condensation

Quick Test

1. Which of these materials will dissolve in water?

   sand   glitter   salt

   bath crystals   gravel   sugar

2. What does water change into when it evaporates?

3. How could you separate salt from water? Describe an experiment.

4. What happens to sugar when it is added to hot coffee?

5. If steam hits a cold surface, what happens?

Reversible changes

Changing materials

We can do things to materials that cause them to change. We can heat them and freeze them, for example. Some changes are reversible – meaning you can change the materials back to what they were in the beginning – but others are not.

Reversible changes

Imagine you are melting some butter, ready to make flapjacks. However, if you took too long to weigh out the other ingredients, the butter would go hard again! Butter melts when it is heated, but when it cools again, it goes hard. This is a **reversible change**. If you made a chocolate cake, you might melt chocolate to spread on the top of the cake. You have to spread the chocolate quickly, because as it cools, it will harden. This is another reversible change.

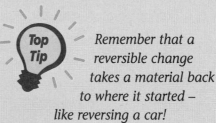

Remember that a reversible change takes a material back to where it started – like reversing a car!

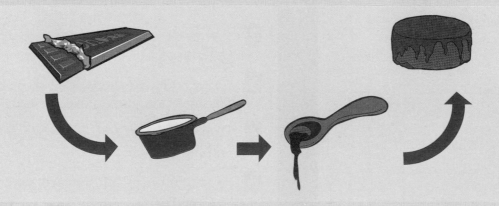

More reversible changes

Imagine you are making ice lollies from fruit juice. You pour the juice into moulds and put them in the freezer. When you get them out later, the lollies are hard. Imagine you leave one on the counter for a while. When you came back, what would you find? A pool of juice! Freezing juice or water is another reversible change.

All this talk of food is making me hungry.

Me too – let's go and make some irreversible changes to the fridge!

Have a go...

Can you explain what happens to each material as it changes?

Try putting chocolate on a plate in the sunshine, then put it in the fridge.

Try leaving butter out on the table in a warm room, then put it in the fridge.

Key words

reversible change

Quick Test

Fill in the missing words from the box below:

hard   melted   water

change   reversible

I left some chocolate in my car and it

1_____. I put it in the fridge

and it went 2_____ again.

So it was a 3_____ change.

When ice melts, it turns back into

4_____. This is also a

reversible 5_____.

Irreversible changes

Changing materials

We know that we can do things to materials to cause them to change. We also know that some changes are reversible – and some are not. **Irreversible changes** are changes that cannot be reversed, like burning wood or frying eggs.

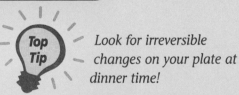

Top Tip Look for irreversible changes on your plate at dinner time!

My favourite example of irreversible change is a fried egg!

And mine is a meringue!

Irreversible changes

An irreversible change is a change that takes place and cannot be reversed to change the material back to its original state. Imagine you are at a bonfire night party. You would be surrounded by all sorts of irreversible changes!

The wood on the bonfire is burning. As it burns, it changes from wood to ash. There is nothing you can do to reverse that change. As the fireworks are lit and they start to burn, they cannot be changed back to their original state.

Imagine you are cooking eggs. As you fry them in the pan, the whites change from a clear, runny material to an opaque, rubbery texture. This is an irreversible change. No matter what, you could not change the eggs back to their original state.

Imagine you are having meringues for pudding. Once the meringue mixture changes in the heat of the oven, from white fluffy foam to a hard crispy shell, it can never be changed back. This is another example of an irreversible change.

Have a go...

Can you think of any other foods that can be changed reversibly or irreversibly as they are cooked? Make a list.

Key words

irreversible change

Quick Test

Put 'R' for reversible or 'I' for irreversible next to each of these changes:

1. Chocolate melting in a pan
2. Butter going soft and runny at a picnic
3. Eggs being poached
4. Ice cubes melting
5. Coal burning

Rock and soil types

Looking at rocks

Rocks can be found everywhere! When you go to the beach, you can see cliffs: these are made of rock. Pebbles on the beach are rocks – and even sand is sometimes made from tiny ground-up pieces of rock. (Sand can also be partly made up of ground-up shells.)

Rock is used for many things.

- houses
- castles
- bridges
- churches
- walls
- pavements and floors
- roofs
- statues and memorials

Rocks can be **classified according to how hard they are**.

Rocks such as **granite** are hard. Granite is used to build things because it is hard and strong.

Chalk is not very hard. It crumbles easily. It would not therefore be a good material for building houses, as the walls would crumble!

The uses of rocks and soils

Rocks and soil are used for many purposes. Houses are built, for example, from stone, bricks, and slate. However, did you know that glass is also a product of rock? It is produced using sand – and sand is rock or shells that have been worn down into tiny particles.

Types of soil

When you think of soil, you probably get a picture in your mind of a dark brown, crumbly substance. However, there are many different types of soil in different places. The colour and properties of the soil depend largely upon the base rock that the soil is made from.

Sandy soil – has a pale colour and water drains through easily.

Clay soil – sticky, orange or blue clay does not drain easily and puddles lie for some time after rain. It dries out with huge cracks on the surface.

Chalky soil – pale colour, drains quickly. It is a thin, poor soil that not many plants are able to grow on.

Peat – this dark, crumbly soil is made from ancient, decayed, plant material rather than rock particles. It holds lots of water.

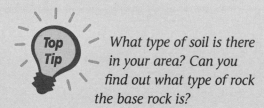

Top Tip *What type of soil is there in your area? Can you find out what type of rock the base rock is?*

See http://www.eais.net/soil/ for more details.

So the soil on my football boots might contain clay?

Which might explain why you stay stuck to the spot and never get the ball!

Have a go...

Can you can talk about different types of soil and their properties? Buy a cheap soil testing kit and find out about the soil in your garden.

Key words

granite   chalk

Quick Test

1 Name three types of soil.

2 Name three types of rock.

3 Which is harder – chalk or granite?

4 What is sand made from?

5 What can affect the type of soil found in a particular place?

Materials that conduct heat

Conducting heat

Some materials **conduct** heat very well.

Think of a metal spoon that has been left in a steaming cup of coffee – it gets very hot indeed! **Metal is a material that conducts heat well**. It is called a **thermal conductor**.

That is why saucepans are made from metal; they heat up quickly. However, the handles are usually made from another material, such as plastic or wood, because they are poor conductors. This means that you are less likely to burn your hands!

Safety

Be careful when you are cooking, as it is easy to get burnt. The metal cooking trays and pans conduct heat well, and this heat can burn your hands. Always use a **thermal insulator**, such as oven gloves, to keep your hands safe!

Now I know why Granddad always talks about wearing his thermals in cold weather!

Mum said it's the layer of trapped air that keeps him warm, YUK!

Thermal insulators

Thermal insulators are materials that keep things warm. Your duvet, fleece coat or woolly socks are good examples of insulators. **Insulators help to prevent heat being lost**. Funnily enough, it is the air in many of these things that makes them good insulators! The inside of a duvet, for example, is filled with feathers or fleecy wadding. These both trap large quantities of air. Cork flooring is also a good insulator for the same reason; it contains a high proportion of trapped air. Wearing layers of clothing, rather than one heavy topcoat, keeps you warmer for the same reason – the trapped air. Air is a poor conductor of heat, so the heat is less likely to be lost through the clothing.

Top Tip *You could use a 'forehead' strip thermometer, or a stick thermometer if you have one, to measure the temperature of water poured into several cups. If not, see which feels the hottest to the touch.*

Have a go...

*Remembering to **always** be careful with hot liquids, put some warm tap water into four plastic cups. Leave one as it is and wrap the others in different materials, such as paper, bubble wrap, cotton wool, fabric. After ten minutes, see which is warmest.*

Key words

conduct

thermal conductor

thermal insulator

Quick Test

1. What is a thermal insulator?
2. Name two materials that are good thermal insulators.
3. What is a thermal conductor?
4. Name a material that is a good thermal conductor.
5. Explain how a duvet keeps you warm.

Test your skills

Be a research scientist!

You are going to carry out an experiment and record your findings just like a professional scientist. You will need:

- An empty two-litre plastic fizzy drink bottle

- An old container and spoon for mixing

- Scissors

- Water

- Sand or fine gravel; if not available use ground coffee (not instant coffee granules)

- Plain white kitchen paper towels

What to do

Carefully cut off the top third of the bottle. Take off the cap and throw it away.

1 Turn the top of the bottle upside down and push it into the other part of the bottle, like in the picture on the right.

2 Press the kitchen towel into the bottle.

3 Mix the sand/grit/coffee with the water.

4 Pour the mixture through the apparatus you have made.

5 What happens? Where is the water? Where is the solid?

6 Write a report, with a diagram, of what you did and the things you found out.

Have a go...

What other mixtures can you separate using a filter? What different materials are filters made from?

Test your knowledge

Section 1

1   Name a material that fits each description:

pliable   _____

opaque   _____

transparent   _____

brittle   _____

2   Mark these materials as thermal conductors (C) or thermal insulators (I):

metal   _____   polystyrene   _____

cork   _____   air   _____

wood   _____

Section 2

1   What process would you use to separate an insoluble solid from a liquid?
_____

2   What process would you use to separate a soluble solid from a liquid?
_____

3   How are rocks used in everyday life?
_____

4   Name three types of rock.

_____

_____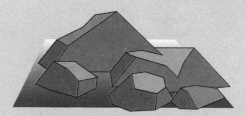

_____

Section 3

1 Draw a diagram of an experiment that could be used to separate salt from water.

2 Give an example of a solid, liquid and gas.

_____

_____

_____

3 Fill in the missing words using the box below:

| vapour | heated | condensation | liquid | gas | state |

When water is _____ it starts to change from a liquid to a

_____. The water has become _____. If

the water vapour hits a cold surface, it changes _____ again,

from a gas to a _____. This is called _____.

I thought that was a bit hard.

I'm hardly surprised!

Forces

Gravity

The Earth pulls things down towards itself with a force called **gravity**. The Earth is very large, and has a great **mass**, so the pull of the Earth's gravity is very strong. It is **gravity that makes things fall when they are dropped**.

Other planets make gravity too, as does the Moon. Have you ever seen film of astronauts on the moon? They bounce about, because the Moon has a weaker gravitational pull than the Earth. This is because the Moon is smaller than the Earth.

In deep space, there is no gravity. Scientists call this **zero gravity**.

Top Tip

Make sure you can explain why things fall to the ground when you drop them.

So if there was no gravity, things would just float away when I drop them?

Might stop you making such a mess!

Friction

Have you ever tried to slide on an icy playground? Did you get far? Do you think you would have managed to slide very far if there had been no ice?

Friction is created when things are pulled past each other. The rougher the surface, the greater the friction created. The smoother the surface, the less friction is created.

Friction helps us to grip the ground with our shoes as we walk. The tread on the soles of your shoes makes them rough and creates friction, even on quite smooth floors.

Have a go...

Try sliding on different surfaces, but be very careful. Can you predict which ones will let you slide the furthest? Can you explain your reasoning?

Key words

gravity	zero gravity
mass	friction

Quick Test

1 If you dropped them at the same time, which of these would fall to the ground first?

 a An orange

 b A marble

 Give a reason for your answer.

2 Which force makes us slow down when we slide?

3 Which has a weaker gravitational pull – the Moon or the Earth?

Electricity

Electricity

We cannot see electricity, but **we can see what it does**. We use **electricity** in the home for **light, heat and cooking**. This electricity is called **mains electricity**. We also use electricity for toys and games, but this is a different, safer type that we get from **a battery**. This is the type of electricity we use for experiments in school and it is perfectly safe.

Electricity is not stored in a battery. **Electricity is made or generated inside the battery** when the chemicals inside react with one another. When a battery has gone flat, it just means that all the chemicals have already reacted with one another – they are all used up. Once there is no more reaction between them, there is no more power.

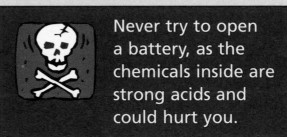

Mains electricity can be very dangerous and can kill you if you do not act sensibly. You should never plug things in or touch switches with wet hands, or you can get an electric shock. For the same reason, never poke anything into a plug socket.

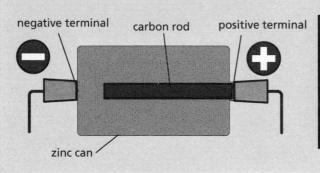

negative terminal   carbon rod   positive terminal

zinc can

Never try to open a battery, as the chemicals inside are strong acids and could hurt you.

Circuit symbols

Circuit symbols are used by scientists to represent pieces of equipment:

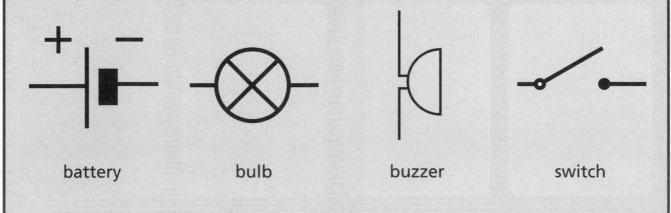

battery   bulb   buzzer   switch

Electrical circuits

Electricity flows through wires like water through a pipe. The battery acts like a pump, pushing the **current** through the wire. If a bulb is connected to a battery by wires in a circuit, the bulb or lamp will light. If the flow of electricity around the circuit is broken, the lamp will not light. A switch may be included in a circuit to break the flow of electricity and turn the bulb on and off.

Metals are good conductors of electricity, so wires are made of copper, a soft metal that can be stretched thin without breaking. Copper wire has a protective coat of plastic, which does not conduct electricity.

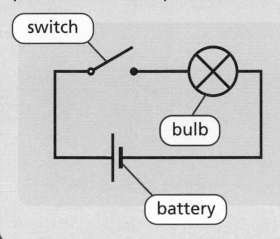

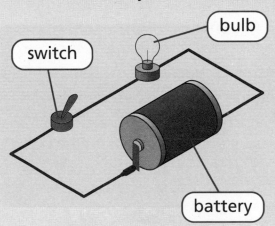

These questions suit my electric personality!

Have a go...

Can you explain to someone how a battery works in a circuit? Find out more at:
http://www.bbc.co.uk/schools/revisewise/science/physical/11_fact.shtml

Key words

electricity	battery
mains electricity	current

Quick Test

1 What do the following circuit symbols stand for?

a    b

2 What sort of materials are good conductors of electricity?

3 Name four things in your home that use mains electricity.

4 Name three things in your home that use battery electricity.

Sound

Sound

Sound is a vibration in the air. Imagine you can hear a guitar being played. The sound you hear is made when the strings vibrate, which causes the air around them to vibrate. The vibrations in the air enter your ear and your eardrum vibrates. This, in turn, makes the tiny bones inside your ear vibrate. A message is sent through a part of your ear, called the **cochlea**, through a nerve to your brain, telling you that you can hear guitar music.

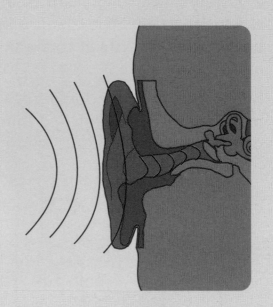

Top Tip

Never put or poke anything in your ear because the eardrum is very delicate and thin, so is easily damaged. If it is damaged, you will be unable to hear properly.

Sound travels in waves

Sound travels through the air in waves. These waves are invisible, but we can see how they might look with a special instrument called an **oscilloscope**. This measures the **amplitude** of the sound. That just means how much energy a sound has or how loud it is.

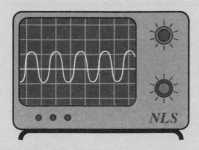

How is sound measured?

Sound is measured in **decibels (dB)**. Very loud sounds can damage your ears. That is why you see people wearing ear mufflers when they are using noisy tools, like pneumatic drills. They muffle the sound and help to prevent damage. Ears can also be damaged by infections and illnesses, although most of these can be treated by the doctor. Wax blocking your ears also affects your hearing, and because the mechanics of the ear age, some people become hard of hearing when they get old.

Sounds good to me!

Sounds lovely and peaceful to me!

Have a go...

Can you explain to someone how we hear sounds? Find out more about sounds – and how they may be changed – at:
http://www.bbc.co.uk/schools/science clips/ages/9_10/changing_sounds.shtml

Key words

vibration	amplitude
cochlea	decibels (dB)
oscilloscope	

Quick Test

1. What unit do we use to measure sound?
2. What does amplitude mean?
3. How can hearing be damaged?
4. What is an oscilloscope?
5. What is the cochlea?

The Earth and beyond

Day, night and seasons

Did you know that the reason why we have day and night and the four seasons is because of the **movement of the Earth as it spins in space?**

The Earth **orbits** around the Sun once every 365 and a quarter days. This is what we call a year. The Moon takes 28 days to orbit the Earth. The seasons are caused by the Earth tilting over as it turns.

When the north of the Earth is tilted towards the Sun, our days in Britain are longer and warmer. This is spring and summer.

When the north of the Earth is tilted away from the sun, we have shorter, colder days – autumn and winter.

Amazing to think we're spinning so fast in space!

As long as we don't spin off!

The sun

It looks to us as though the Sun moves across the sky during the day. The Sun does not move; it is the Earth that moves.

sunrise	midday	sunset
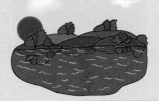		
As the Sun rises, we see it in the east.	At midday, the Sun is at its highest in the sky. This makes shadows look very short as the Sun is shining directly overhead.	The Sun then seems to 'set' or 'go down' in the west.

Top Tip *Make sure you can draw on a **diagram** the position of the Sun in the early morning, at midday and as the Sun sets – it is a favourite with examiners!*

Have a go...

Measure shadows at different points in the day – early morning, lunchtime and in the evening. Mark the outline of the shadow you have chosen on the floor with chalk and then compare them. You can see how the Earth rotates.

Key words

orbits   diagram

Quick Test

1 What causes the seasons?

2 During which part of the day is the Sun at its highest in the sky?

3 Is it the Sun or the Earth that moves during the day?

4 Do you see the Sun set in the west or the east?

5 How long does it take for the Earth to orbit the Sun?

Magnets

Attraction and repulsion

Have you ever heard the phrase, 'opposites attract'? In the case of magnets, that is absolutely true! **Magnets have a north pole and a south pole**. If you put the north pole of one magnet next to the south pole of another magnet, the magnets will be attracted to each other and will pull together. If you put two south or north poles together, they will **repel** and try to push away from each other.

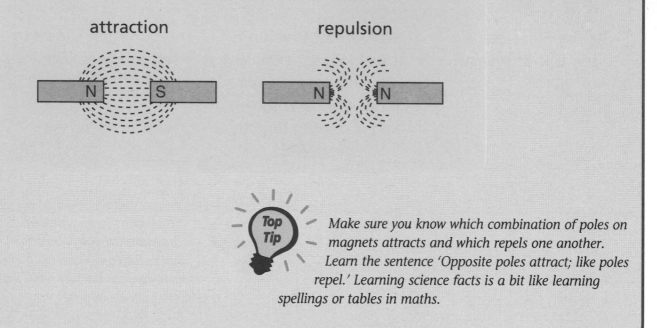

attraction

repulsion

Make sure you know which combination of poles on magnets attracts and which repels one another. Learn the sentence 'Opposite poles attract; like poles repel.' Learning science facts is a bit like learning spellings or tables in maths.

What materials do magnets attract?

Magnets attract metals containing iron, such as steel. They also attract cobalt and nickel. Have you ever played a game using magnets? There is a game where a magnet on a string attached to a pole is used to catch 'fish' with metal tips. The game uses magnets and the attraction of metal to magnets. You can make your own game using pictures you have drawn and cut out, with metal paper clips attached. Make a pole with a pencil, string and a magnet.

Magnets work through materials

Magnets can work through other materials, depending on the strength of the magnet and the thickness of the material.

A magnet can attract an object through paper or card, for example. You can test this by placing paper clips on paper or card and moving them around invisibly with a magnet underneath.

Opposites attract? That must be why I like Sam, then...

Yuk!!

Have a go...

Using magnets to attract through other materials can be fun. For example, you could make a spooky haunted house scene where ghosts, furniture – whatever you like – move invisibly... with a little help from your magnet!

Key words

pole   **repel**

Quick Test

1 Which of these materials will be attracted to a magnet?

> iron filings   plastic pen lid
>
> leaf   paper clip   pebble
>
> chalk   drawing pin   jelly sweet
>
> sewing needle

2 Fill in the missing words from the box below:

> south   north   attract   repel
>
> attract   repel

Magnets have a _____ pole and a _____ pole. When two south poles or two north poles are held near each other they will _____. This is because two like magnets will always _____ one another. When a north and south pole are held near each other, they will _____ because opposites always _____.

Light

Sources of light

We see things because **light is given off by an object or reflected by it**. However, people are sometimes confused about whether a thing is a light source or is just reflecting the light.

The Sun is a **source of light**, because it makes light; it is a burning ball of fire. The Moon is more confusing because we talk about the Moon 'shining' – but in fact, all the Moon does is reflect light – the light given off by the Sun.

A lamp is a source of light and so is a torch. They actually make light.

A fire is a source of light, for the same reason, and so is a candle.

Other things seem to shine so brightly that it would be easy to get confused. A mirror, glass, glittery surfaces, metals and tin foil all shine – but they are not sources of light. They are just very good **reflectors**. This is because they have very smooth, shiny surfaces.

Top Tip

If you cannot decide whether an object is a light source or a reflector, try to imagine what it would do if you shut it in a dark box. Would it glow? If it would, then it is a source of light!

Does light bend?

Light travels in straight lines. We can see evidence of this when we look at a **shadow**. Since light cannot bend around objects, the light blocked by an object shows up as a shadow. We see light travelling in straight lines clearly at night when we use a torch, or the headlights on a car, or see the beam of light that shines out of a lighthouse.

When light hits an object, it bounces off and enters our eyes. This is how we see things.

I need some new reflectors on my bike to help me be seen at night.

The way you ride, I'd buy some floodlights!

Have a go...

Look at this great website to find some activities you can carry out to find out more about light:
http://acept.la.asu.edu/PiN/act/activities.shtml

Key words

source of light   shadow

reflector

Quick Test

1 Which of these things are sources of light?

> sun   moon   water   mirror
> headlight   television screen
> tin foil   copper pan

2 Make a list of five sources of light in and around your home.

Test your skills

Make a singing balloon!

What you need:

- 1 big round balloon
- 1 small coin

What to do

- Stretch the neck of the balloon and poke the coin inside.

- Blow up the balloon. Be careful – you don't want to get the coin in your mouth!

- Tie the balloon neck to trap the air and the coin inside.

- Hold the balloon between your hands and move it in circles. You need to make the coin start to roll on its edge around the inside of the balloon.

- Put your ear on the balloon and listen. What can you hear?

- Does the sound change at all as the coin slows down and falls over?

What is happening?

When the coin moves fast, it causes the balloon to vibrate quickly. Objects vibrating quickly make a high-pitched sound. As the coin slows down, the pitch of the sound gets lower. Clever, isn't it?

Can you invent another investigation to explore how sound works?

Well, Mel proves this theory right! She charges about quickly and makes high-pitched noises...!

And you just blow out hot air!

Have a go...

Would using a bigger or smaller coin in this experiment change anything? Have a try!

Test your knowledge

Section 1

Draw a circuit diagram that contains:

- a bulb
- a switch
- 2 batteries

Section 2

1 How does friction help us to stay upright on an icy morning?

_____

2 What force stops us from floating off into space?

_____

3 What unit is used to measure sound?

_____

4 What would happen if you put the north poles of two magnets near each other?

_____

5 What would happen if you put the south poles of two magnets near each other?

_____

6 What would happen if you put the north and south poles of two magnets together?

_____

Section 3

Ring the pictures below that show a source of light.

Section 4

1 What do scientists mean when they talk about there being 'zero gravity' in space? What are the effects of zero gravity?

_____

2 How do we hear things?

_____

3 Can light travel around objects?

_____

4 How are shadows made?

_____

5 Are these substances solid (S), liquid (L) or gas (G)?

water _____   ice _____

milk _____   carbon dioxide _____

steam _____   cheese _____

oxygen _____   chalk _____

About the Tests

The tests in Science

The tests in Science take place alongside the tests for English and Maths in May of each year. The tests are designed to show how much you have learnt during your time at primary school – not just how much you have learnt in Year 6!

You will be tested on many different topics, covering all areas of the National Curriculum for Science. That means you will find questions on life and the living processes of plants, animals and humans; materials such as rocks and soils; and physical processes such as electricity, forces and magnetism.

Questions will also test your ability to read data such as graphs and your knowledge of investigations and how to set up experiments. These topics are all covered in this book.

Your teachers will also assess your work, and the results of these assessments, and your tests, will be reported to your parents in July.

Although your results are used in League Tables, these tables are just to show how well your primary school is doing, compared to other schools. The results of your tests are not considered when a secondary school offers you a place, but they may use the results to help to put you in your first teaching groups in the core subjects of Science, Maths and English.

Levels of achievement

The National Curriculum divides up work into eight levels. By Year 6, you are expected to reach about Level 4. The General Science papers themselves will test all abilities from Level 3 to Level 5. The papers A and B each carry the same amount of marks and last 45 minutes.

Preparing for the tests

The most important thing you can do is KEEP CALM! These tests are important, but do not get worried about them. You can only do your best and if you have listened in class and worked your way through this book, you will be very well prepared indeed!

Make sure you have lots of rest and spend time relaxing with your friends just before the tests. There is no point cramming the night before, but a quick read over the notes you have made, together with this book, will help to reassure you that you are prepared.

Remember – important though they are, the results of your KS2 Tests will soon be in the past as you start your exciting new career at secondary school!

Make sure you are eating healthily and taking time for fun exercise in the run up to your tests – a game of football or basketball will get your heart rate up (as you should know from reading this book!) and the exercise will make you feel good, as well as helping you to relax. Make sure you have breakfast on the day of the test – porridge is a really good idea, or wholemeal toast, or yoghurt with fruit. Anything with slow burning carbohydrates, like the foods mentioned above, will help, because they release energy slowly and keep you supplied with it for longer. Ask if you will be able to take a bottle of water in with you too, as staying hydrated will help you to concentrate too.

Test practice

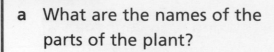

Plants

a What are the names of the parts of the plant?

1 _____

2 _____

3 _____

4 _____

b What is the function or job of each part?
Join the correct label to each name:

leaf   root   stem   petal

| to attract pollinating insects with smell and colour | to hold the flowers up in the air for pollination and to carry water to all parts of the plant | to anchor the plant in the soil and draw up water and nutrients | where the plant makes food using light from the sun |

c What do most plants need to grow? Circle the correct answers:

water   wind   salt   light   beetles   nutrients

the correct temperature   a cool temperature

d How are seeds dispersed or spread? Name four ways:

_____   _____

_____   _____

Habitats

a Look at the habitats and animals in the pictures below. Match the animal to the correct habitat and describe two ways in which each animal has adapted.

Desert _____

Seashore _____

Tropical forest _____

Antarctic _____

b Draw arrows to show the direction in which energy flows along this food chain.

c Which living thing in the food chain is the producer?

_____

d Which is the primary consumer?

_____

e Which is the top carnivore?

_____

Materials

a Look at the table below. It shows some of the materials you may find in your home, what they are used for and why those particular materials were chosen: their properties. Unfortunately, the table has got mixed up. Can you use a line to join each material with what it has been used for and why it was chosen? The first one has been done for you.

material	use	properties
stone	windows	conducts heat well
wood	window frames	transparent – you can see through it
plastic	cushion covers	easy to clean; hygienic
fabric	saucepans	soft and warm to touch
glass	walls	strong and secure
metal	food storage boxes	strong, but light and easy to cut to size

b Which of these materials are natural and which are synthetic (made by people)?

chalk _____

plastic _____

leather _____

polystyrene _____

wood _____

Give reasons for your answers.

_____

_____

_____

_____

_____

_____

Life processes

a There are seven life processes that all living things share, but what does each word mean?

Match the words to the correct meaning:

nutrition	get rid of waste
locomotion	produce young
sensitivity	feed
respiration	move
excretion	breathe
maturation	feel things
reproduction	grow and change

b Which of these things are alive? Draw a circle round them.

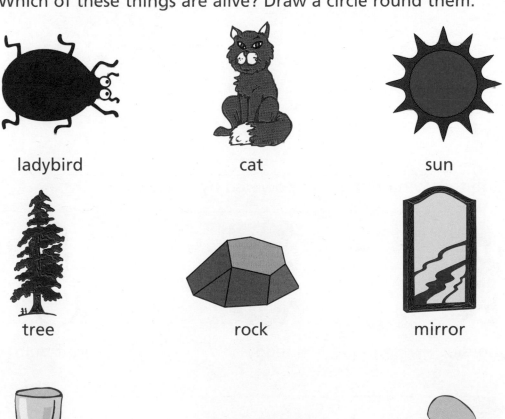

ladybird   cat   sun

tree   rock   mirror

glass   dog   rain

Physical processes

a Which of these circuits will light the bulb? Tick the complete circuits.

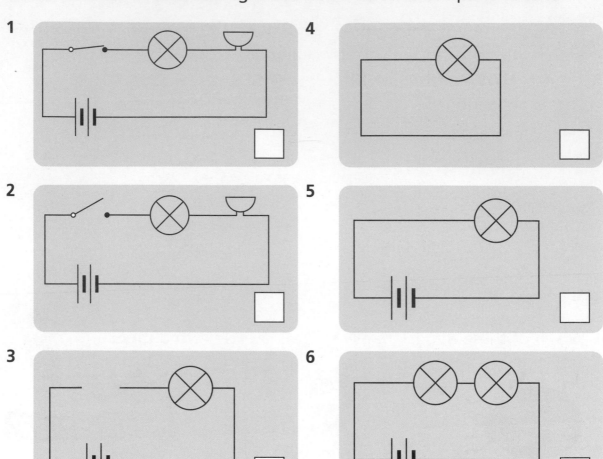

1

4

2

5

3

6

b Which of the following things are powered by electricity?

toy soldier

teddy

light bulb

games console

remote control car

book

Plants

PAGES 4–5 FLOWERING PLANTS

1 root

2 petal

3 leaf

4 male

5 female

PAGES 6–7 A TRANSFER OF ENERGY

1 water, light

2 photosynthesis

3 a green chemical in leaves that helps the process of photosynthesis

4 plump, but yellow leaves

5 crinkly and dry; brown – then dead!

PAGES 8–9 HOW PLANTS REPRODUCE

1 pollination, fertilisation, seed dispersion, germination

2 a true

  b false

  c true

3 moisture, air and the correct temperature

4 Any three of the following ways are correct: animals and birds eating the seeds, gripping onto the fur or feathers, travelling by water, being blown by the wind and by the seed pods exploding.

5 the process carried out by insects or the wind as pollen is carried from one plant to another

PAGES 12–13 TEST YOUR KNOWLEDGE

Section 1

1 petal

2 stem

3 leaf

4 pollen

5 root

Section 2

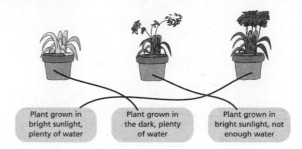

Section 3

circled items are:

1 moisture air correct temperature

2 insects wind

3 wind water birds animals explosions

Animals and ecosystems

PAGES 14–15 GROWING AND CHANGING

1 when a creature undergoes a complete physical change from child to adult

2 any four appropriate answers such as frogs, ladybirds, dragonflies and newts

3 frog spawn

4 frog spawn, tadpole, froglet, frog

PAGES 16–17 USING CLASSIFICATION KEYS

See page 16 for help.

PAGES 18–19 FOOD CHAINS

1 sun, seaweed, cod, shark

2 1 → d, 2 → a, 3 → c, 4 → b

PAGES 20–21 ANIMALS IN THEIR ENVIRONMENT

child's design for their own alien, adapted to the environment on planet Plaaarp

PAGES 22–23 LIVING PROCESSES

cat, cactus, spider

PAGES 24–25 MICROORGANISMS

1 by breaking down waste and in the production of beer, bread and yoghurt.

2 viruses, bacteria and fungi

3 measles, flu or mumps

4 any sensible answer – could be stomach upset, ear infection, etc.

5 any sensible answer – yoghurt, for instance

PAGES 26–27 LOOKING AT HABITATS

1 → a   4 → c

2 → e   5 → d

3 → b

PAGES 30–31 TEST YOUR KNOWLEDGE

Section 1

1 A habitat is the place where organisms such as plants and animals live – the seashore, woods and rainforests are examples.

2 A community is the collection of plants and animals that live in a particular habitat.

3 An ecosystem is the name given to a community and its environment.

Section 2

1
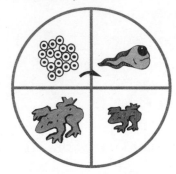

2 metamorphosis

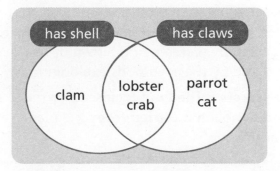

Section 3

✔ Thick, waterproof fur
✔ Wide tail like a paddle
✔ Large front teeth for gnawing wood

Section 4

has shell | has claws

clam | lobster crab | parrot cat

Section 5

fungus → mouldy bread

bacteria → gastroenteritis

virus → flu

Humans

PAGES 32–33 THE CIRCULATORY SYSTEM

1 red cells, white cells, platelets, plasma
2 four
3 The blood in an artery is under lots of pressure so it spurts out of any cuts.
4 white
5 liquid containing salts, sugars, proteins

PAGES 34–35 LOOKING AT TEETH

1 → c
2 → a
3 → b
4 incisors and molars
5 canines

PAGES 36–37 LOOKING AT BONES

1 support, protection and movement
2 skull, shoulder blade, spine and pelvis
3 biceps, triceps
4 the brain
5 heart, lungs

PAGES 38–39 EATING HEALTH FOOD

A picnic to include foods from all the groups, i.e. protein, fat, carbohydrate, fibre.

PAGES 42–43 TEST YOUR KNOWLEDGE

Section 1

1 fats, carbohydrate, protein, fibre, water, vitamins and minerals

2

Raw and unprocessed foods contain the most vitamins and the least sugar, salt and other additives, so are always the healthiest option.

3 to help us to digest our food
4 any combination that only includes small quantities of sweets, crisps and fizzy drinks

Section 2

1 for grinding tough plants
2 for killing prey and tearing meat
3 (incisor) indicator omnivores
   (molar) mole molecular
   (canine) ceramic capillaries
4 support, movement, protection
5 red cells, white cells, plasma, platelets
6 Red cells carry **oxygen** around the body. White blood cells attack **microbes** and fight disease.

Materials

PAGES 44–45 LOOKING AT MATERIALS

1 plastic, metal, cotton, paper, leather, wood, china
2 See pages 44 and 45 for help.

PAGES 46–47 FILTRATION

1 insoluble

2 filtration
3 a labelled diagram of the equipment, showing funnel, filter paper and beaker

PAGES 48–49 MATERIALS THAT DISSOLVE

1 salt, bath crystals, sugar
2 steam, water vapour

3 through evaporation and condensation. I would heat the salt water mixture and have something cool above it for the water to condense on.

4 It dissolves.

5 It condenses.

PAGES 50–51 REVERSIBLE CHANGES

1 melted

2 hard

3 reversible

4 water

5 change

PAGES 52–53 IRREVERSIBLE CHANGES

1 R

2 R

3 I

4 R

5 I

PAGES 54–55 ROCK AND SOIL TYPES

1 any sensible answer including: sandy, clay, peat, chalky

2 any sensible answer including: chalk, granite, marble, limestone, sandstone

3 granite

4 tiny particles of rock or shell

5 the rock underneath – the base rock

PAGES 56–57 MATERIALS THAT CONDUCT HEAT

1 something that helps prevent heat loss

2 feathers, fleece

3 something that conducts heat very well

4 metal

5 Feathers trap air in the duvet. The trapped air heats up and cannot escape so it keeps you warm using your own trapped body heat.

PAGES 60–61 TEST YOUR KNOWLEDGE

Section 1

1 any suitable materials including:
pliable – rubber
opaque – wood
transparent – glass
brittle – some plastics, chalk

2 metal – C   polystyrene – I
cork – I   air – I
wood – I

Section 2

1 filtration

2 evaporation

3 building walls, roofs, houses, paving, churches, etc.

4 any sensible answer including chalk, granite, marble, limestone, sandstone

Section 3

1

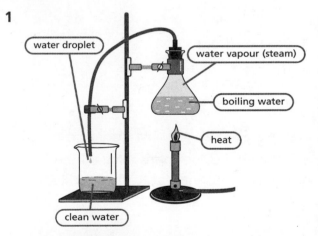

2 many answers are possible, for instance:
solid: **stone**
liquid: **water**
gas: **air**

3 When water is **heated** it starts to change from a liquid to a **gas**. The water has become **vapour**. If the water vapour hits a cold surface, it changes **state** again, from a gas to a **liquid**. This is called **condensation**.

Physical processes

PAGES 62–63 FORCES

1 Both would fall at the same rate, because gravity affects them equally.

2 friction

3 moon

PAGES 64–65 ELECTRICITY

1 a bulb

  b battery

2 metals

3 any sensible answer such as lights, cooker, microwave, etc.

4 any sensible answer such as toy, torch, etc.

PAGES 66–67 SOUND

1 decibels (dB)

2 how much energy a sound has

3 very loud sounds, ear infections and illnesses

4 an instrument used to measure the amplitude of sound

5 the part of the ear that sound travels through, so we 'hear' sound

PAGES 68–69 THE EARTH AND BEYOND

1 the Earth tilting over as it turns

2 midday

3 the Earth

4 west

5 365 and a quarter days

PAGES 70–71 MAGNETS

1 iron filings, paper clip, drawing pin, sewing needle

2 north, south, repel, repel, attract, attract

PAGES 72–73 LIGHT

1 sun, headlight, television screen

2 any appropriate answers such as lamp, television, candle, etc.

PAGES 76–77 TEST YOUR KNOWLEDGE

Section 1

any circuit diagram that contains a bulb, a switch and two batteries

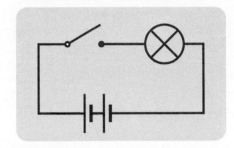

Section 2

1 Friction helps our feet to grip the ground so we do not slip.

2 gravity

3 decibels (dB)

4 They would repel.

5 They would repel.

6 They would attract.

Section 3

Section 4

1 Zero gravity means that there is no gravitational pull, so things float off into space.

2 Sounds are vibrations in the air. The vibrations cause our eardrum to vibrate. The small bones in our ear move and our nerves send a message to our brain telling it we have heard a sound.

3 No – it travels in straight lines.

4 Shadows are made when objects block the light. Light cannot bend, so the shadow shows up where the light has been blocked.

5 water – L   ice – S
milk – L   carbon dioxide – G
steam – G   cheese – S
oxygen – G   chalk – S

Test practice

PAGE 80 PLANTS

a 1 leaf **2** root **3** petals **4** stem

b petal → to attract pollinating insects with smell and colour
stem → to hold the flowers up in the air for pollination and to carry water to all parts of the plant
root → to anchor the plant in the soil and draw up water and nutrients
leaf → where the plant makes food using light from the sun

c circled items are: water, light, nutrients, the correct temperature

d wind, animals, birds, water, explosions

PAGE 81 HABITATS

a Desert – camel – humps to store fat, leathery eyelids and long silky eyelashes to keep out sand, splayed feet for walking on sand

Seashore – anemone – retractable tentacles for sifting water for food means the creature can take shelter from the drying sun and wind when it is exposed by the tide. Its rubbery foot helps it grip the stones and not be washed away by the waves

Tropical forest – spider monkey – toes for gripping and agile fingers for gathering food. Tail long and flexible for gripping trees

Antarctic – penguin – downy underfeathers to keep it warm, waterproof outer feathers to keep it dry. Streamlined shape for swimming

b sun → pondweed → tadpole → heron

c pondweed or weed

d tadpole

e heron

PAGE 82 MATERIALS

a Stone → walls → strong and secure
wood → window frames → strong, but light and easy to cut to size
plastic → food storage boxes → easy to clean; hygienic
fabric → cushion covers → soft and warm to touch
glass → windows → transparent – you can see through it
metal → saucepans → conducts heat well

b chalk – natural
plastic – synthetic
leather – natural
polystyrene – synthetic
wood – natural

Chalk is a stone, leather is animal skin and wood is from trees.

PAGE 83 LIFE PROCESSES

a nutrition → feed
locomotion → move
sensitivity → feel things
respiration → breathe
excretion → get rid of waste
maturation → grow and change
reproduction → produce young

b Circled items are: ladybird, cat, tree, dog.

PAGE 84 PHYSICAL PROCESSES

a ✔ circuit 1 – cell, bulb, buzzer and closed switch
✔ circuit 5 – cell, bulb
✔ circuit 6 – cell, two bulbs

b light bulb, games console, remote control car

adapt the way in which plants and animals change over time to cope with the conditions in their environment

amplitude how loud a sound is; a loud sound such as a shout has a high amplitude, and a quiet sound such as a whisper has a low amplitude

artery a blood vessel that carries blood away from the heart

bacteria tiny microorganisms that can cause an illness such as gastroenteritis, or be helpful like the bacteria that turn milk into yoghurt

battery a source of energy, created by a chemical reaction

biceps the large bulgy muscle on the upper side of your upper arm

brittle materials that are stiff and break easily, e.g. glass

camouflage a disguise to match an environment; a leopard's spots hide the animal in the dappled light of the jungle

canine the sharp, pointy teeth used for tearing food

carbohydrate a food group that includes foods such as pasta and cereals

carnivore an animal that eats meat, i.e. other animals

cells tiny building blocks that make up all living things – plants and animals

chalk a soft rock; crumbles easily

characteristics features such as colour and size

chlorophyll a green chemical found in plants that helps them to make food using the energy in sunlight

circulatory system the system of blood vessels such as arteries and veins that carries blood round the body

classification the process used (by scientists) to sort things into sets

classification key a key used to sort plants and creatures into groups

cochlea the shell-shaped part inside the ear that helps us to hear sounds

community the creatures and plants that live together in a particular habitat

GLOSSARY

condensation when steam hits a cold surface it changes state from a gas to a liquid and turns back into water – the water is called condensation

conductor an electrical conductor is a material that allows electricity to pass through it; a thermal conductor is a material that allows heat to pass through it

current a flow of electricity

dB the symbol that stands for the unit that measures sound – decibels

decibels the unit that sound is measured in

diagram a scientific drawing

digestive system the system made up of internal organs such as the stomach and intestines that is used to break down food inside the body

dissolve when a solid combines with a liquid and cannot be seen (i.e. salt or sugar in water)

ecology the study of living things in their surroundings

ecosystem a community of plants and animals and its environment

electricity a source of energy transported by wires and stored in batteries

energy what is used whenever work is done, e.g. food gives you chemical energy. Other forms of energy include sound, heat, light and electrical energy

environment the natural surroundings of an animal or plant

evaporation a process where a liquid changes state into a gas

fair test a test where everything is judged to be equal at the start of an experiment – except the particular thing being tested for

fats a food group that includes butter and nuts

fertilisation when the male and female cells join together to make a new life, the process is called fertilisation; this happens with plants and animals

fibre found in foods such as cereal, fruit and vegetables; it is bulky and indigestible in itself, but helps us to digest other foods

filtration a process used to separate soluble and insoluble materials, e.g. sand and water

food chain shows the way in which energy is passed from the sun to plants, which are then eaten by animals, who are in turn eaten by other animals

92

food web similar to food chains, but show much more complicated feeding relationships

friction the rubbing together of moving objects that slows them down

fungi plants that do not make energy using sunlight, but instead absorb the goodness made when other plants and animals decay

germination when a seed starts to grow

granite a hard rock; good for building with

gravity the force that makes objects fall to the ground when you drop them; everything in the universe is attracted to everything else by gravity

habitat the place where plants and animals live is called a habitat, e.g. the seashore and woodland

herbivore an animal that is totally vegetarian, e.g. a cow

hinge joint a joint of the body that works like a door hinge, e.g. knee or elbow

incisor front teeth, which are used for biting into our food; rabbits have large incisors for cropping grass

insoluble materials that will not dissolve, e.g. sand is insoluble In water

internal organs organs inside our body such as our heart and kidneys

irreversible change a change that cannot be reversed, such as an egg being fried or wood being burnt

larva the young (baby) of an insect before it has changed into adult form

leaf the food factory where a plant uses sunlight to make energy

life cycle describes the changes and growth an organism goes through from birth to adulthood

light energy given off by anything luminous such as street lights, candles and fires

mains electricity the electricity that we use in the home when we plug something into a wall socket

mass the amount of matter that something contains; how heavy an object is depends on its mass

materials what things are made of, e.g. plastic or wood

metamorphosis when a creature undergoes a complete physical change when growing from child to adult, e.g. a caterpillar becoming a butterfly

microorganisms tiny organisms such as bacteria and viruses

mnemonic a silly sentence made up to jog your memory, e.g. the sentence 'Richard Of York Gave Battle In Vain' is used to remind people of the order of colours in a rainbow – Red, Orange, Yellow, Green, Blue, Indigo, Violet

molars the back teeth used for grinding food

nutrients the goodness in food eaten (or in the case of plants, in the soil) is known as nutrients; this would include vitamins and minerals

opaque things that do not let light through – and we cannot see through – are opaque, e.g. black sugar paper, for example

orbit the journey made by a planet or asteroid around another planet or star

organism a living thing

oscilloscope a piece of equipment used to measure sound waves

ovary holds eggs – female cells – in animals and plants

petal the part of a plant that is brightly coloured and sometimes scented to attract insects to plants

photosynthesis the name of the process used by plants to change light energy into food

plaque sticky material that causes tooth decay if it is not cleaned away; formed by bacteria acting on food fragments

plasma the clear fluid full of salts that makes up a large part of the blood

platelets the tiny pieces of blood cell that help to make blood clot

pliable materials that are bendy and do not snap easily

pole magnets have a north pole and a south pole

pollen a powdery substance held on the male part of the flower

pollination the name of the process carried out by insects or the wind as pollen is carried from one plant to another

predators animals which hunt and eat other animals are called predators

primary consumer the name given to herbivores in a food chain – animals that eat plants, the primary producers

primary producer plants are producers in the food chain; they use the energy from the sun to make or produce food

properties (of materials) features such as hard/soft/heavy/strong

protein found in foods such as cheese and beans; the body needs this food group for growth and repair

puberty the stage of human development when a child starts to develop into an adult

pulse the beating you feel in your wrist or neck that shows how fast your blood is flowing around your body; after you have exercised, your pulse rate is quicker than normal, as your heart is beating faster

pupa the stage of an insect changing from a larva to an adult during metamorphosis

red cells cells found in the blood that carry dissolved oxygen around the body

reflect, reflected, reflection when light or heat bounces back off a surface, we say that it has been reflected

repel to push away from; two north poles or south poles on magnets will repel each other

reversible change a change that can be reversed, such as melting ice being frozen again

root the part of a plant that anchors it in the soil

secondary consumer a secondary consumer is the animal in a food chain that eats primary consumers; in the food chain lettuce – slug – hedgehog, the hedgehog is the secondary consumer

seed dispersal the way in which seeds are spread out or scattered by the wind, animals, water, explosions or birds

shadow made when light is blocked by an opaque object; shadows are the absence of light

soluble something that dissolves, e.g. salt and sugar are soluble in water

source of light something that gives off light and does not merely reflect it, e.g. the Sun

species a group of similar animals which can breed with one another, such as different types or breeds of cat

stem (plant) the stalk of a flower that holds the flower up, so it can be pollinated by insects or the wind; acts as a pipe, carrying water and nutrients to all parts of the plant

tertiary consumer the top carnivore in a food chain; not eaten by anything else in the chain, e.g. in the chain seaweed – scallop – penguin – walrus – orca whale, the tertiary consumer is the orca whale

thermal conductor a material that allows heat to pass through easily, e.g. metal

thermal insulator a material that does not allow heat to pass through it easily, e.g. wood

transparent a transparent material allows light to pass through it; because of this we can see through transparent materials, e.g. glass

triceps the muscle on the underside of your upper arm

veins the blood vessels that carry blood back to your heart

Venn diagram a diagram made from two circles to show how items may be grouped or classified according to characteristics they share

vibration a quick shaking backwards and forwards movement, e.g. sounds cause the air to vibrate

virus a microorganism that causes illnesses such as flu and the common cold

water vapour another name for steam; type of gas

white cells the defence system of the body; found in the blood, they fight bacteria and viruses

zero gravity the scientific term for there being no gravity in deep space